23. Octobier 2018

Dear Wai

Hap[py]

We love you [thank] you

for being YOU.

Beate, Misha, Jamosh

MILA

The
Things
Trees
Know

written and illustrated by

Douglas Wood

 A Wind In The Pines book

Adventure Publications
Cambridge, Minnesota

Dedicated...

To those who *see* trees.

Illustrations by Douglas Wood
Book design by Jonathan Norberg

Copyright 2005 by Douglas Wood

10 9 8 7 6 5

Published by Adventure Publications
An imprint of AdventureKEEN
(800) 678-7006
www.adventurepublications.net
Printed in China

ISBN: 978-1-59193-130-0

3

To the Reader:

Of all the teachers I have known, I've found none greater than trees.

Having a rough time? Trouble coping with all that Life's throwing at you — storms, drought, hardship, loss? Need a little inspiration? Some advice? Go sit under a tree. An old one, gnarled, with missing limbs, twists, turns, and knotholes.

Still haven't got it? Sit some more. Lay your head against a great root and fall asleep — to the lullaby of wind through leaves or needles. Wake up to the sight of blue sky – or clouds or sun or moon – through a tracery of branches.

If your troubles remain, try the same thing tomorrow, and as often as you can. You will find a generous measure of wisdom, and of peace. It worked for Buddha, after all, and for countless seekers of many cultures and many times.

I remember vividly the night I walked a country road, feeling very low. There were stars in the sky but the night seemed black, and life itself devoid of hope and promise. Then I caught the silhouette of a spreading oak against the stars, and in an instant I knew something important, something that trees know: When life is hard and you're not sure what to do, reach. Reach for the light, reach for where you're rooted. Survive and endure. *Grow* – through whatever hardship comes your way. Stay rooted and strive. Even if you never grasp your goals (what tree actually reaches the sun?) You will attain something greater – your true self. You will fulfill yourself and somehow add something of value and beauty to the world.

And how long should you go on doing this? Only for as long as you live.

> *I have learned a lot from trees:*
> *sometimes about the weather,*
> *sometimes about animals,*
> *sometimes about the Great Spirit.*

- Walking Buffalo

> **These trees shall be my books.**

-William Shakespeare

Reach down as well as up.
No roots, no branches.

Stand tall.
But bend when you need to.

Be a shelter to someone.

*Grow from the bottom up,
from the inside out.*

14

Welcome rainy days.

16

Know that being beautiful is
the same thing as
being yourself.

Reach for the light.

Release the light you've found.

Respect your elders.

Go ahead, get big!

Make fresh air,
not hot air.

Know that the brightest blossoms are not always on the tallest trees.

*Don't let things
eat away at you.*

Want green and living thoughts?
Stand in a green and living wood.

Be well acquainted with the moonlight.

*Know that to attain the sun
is simply to go on seeking it.*

Keep your head in the clouds
and your feet on the ground.
Most of the time.

Know that big trees are just little trees that kept going.

It's simple:
If you're living, you're growing.
If you're growing, you're living.

Remember…
Dreams are the seedlings of Realities.
And it is often from the fertile soil
of failure that they grow.

Give your fruits freely.

Keep a green tree in your heart
And the singing bird will come.

47

Touch the wind, but let it go.
Touch the earth, and hold on tight.

Grow where you're planted.

*Sometimes all there is to do
is endure.*

Sun, storm, drought:
let these sculptors do their work.

Your work is to grow.

Each life becomes a part
of the landscape.
It becomes someone's landmark.

All trees fall,
but Life doesn't end,
it only changes.
The fallen tree keeps giving,
and in all that grows around it,
rises once more.